Classroom Crack-ups!

Based on the TV series *SpongeBob SquarePants* created by
Stephen Hillenburg as seen on Nickelodeon

Stephen Hillenburg

SIMON AND SCHUSTER
First published in Great Britain in 2007 by Simon & Schuster UK Ltd
1st Floor, 222 Gray's Inn Road, London, WC1X 8HB
A CBS Company

Originally published in the USA in 2006 by Simon Spotlight,
an imprint of Simon & Schuster Children's Division, New York.

A CIP catalogue record for this book is available from the British Library

ISBN-13: 978-1-8473-8007-4

Printed and bound in Great Britain by Cox & Wyman Ltd, Reading, Berks

5 7 9 10 8 6 4

Classroom Crack-ups!

by David Lewman

SIMON AND SCHUSTER

Why did Mrs Puff become a teacher?

She's a classy lady.

Where did Sandy go before kindergarten?

Tree school.

Where did Squidward go before kindergarten?

Pre-scowl.

Mrs Puff: Why did the cow study all night?

Sandy: She wanted to go to the head of the grass.

Squidward: What did the drinking fountain say to the student?

SpongeBob: "Have a nice spray."

How does SpongeBob get to the second floor of the school?

He takes the square way.

What's big and lives in the water and works great on blackboards?
The Chalk Ness Monster

Sandy: Why did Patrick punch the library?
SpongeBob: His teacher told him to hit the books

SpongeBob: When is a postbox like the alphabet?

Squidward: When it's full of letters.

SpongeBob: What comes right after taking attendance?

Patrick: Taking an eleven dance.

7

You were right Spongebob! Those jokes are funny! Come on over to the Freedome tomorrow and celebrate. ♡ Sandy

Mr Krabs: What kind of ship must all students master?

Mrs Puff: Penmanship.

Patrick: What kind of pen is not good for writing?

Sandy: A pigpen.

SpongeBob: Why are skeletons so good at maths?

The Flying Dutchman: They really bone up on it.

Why did the student take lipstick and eye shadow to school?

He had to take a make-up test.

SpongeBob: What's the best kind of pen when you're lost in the desert?

Sandy: A fountain pen.

Why did Patrick hit the test with a tennis racket?

He wanted to ace the exam.

What did Mr Krabs say when he found an ancient bug in the dictionary?

"Why, that's the oldest tick in the book."

SpongeBob: Why wouldn't the teacher show his students how to connect two points?

Pearl: That's where he drew the line.

Did SpongeBob complete writing the letter *i* on time?
Yes, he finished right on the dot.

Patrick: Knock-knock.
Squidward: Who's there?
Patrick: Reese.
Squidward: Reese who?
Patrick: Recess is my favourite subject!

Patrick: Why was the soap always good in school?

SpongeBob: He never got in bubble.

Sandy: Where's the best place on a baseball field to take a test?

SpongeBob: Right field.

Mrs Puff: What comes just before detention?

Patrick: C-tention.

What kind of test does Bubble Buddy hate the most?

Pop quizzes.

SpongeBob: Which part of the beach is the smartest?

Pearl: The quicksand.

Sandy: Why did Patrick put his test in his piggy bank?

SpongeBob: He wanted to save it for a brainy day.

Patrick: Knock-knock.
SpongeBob: Who's there?
Patrick: Scram.
SpongeBob: Scram who?
Patrick: Let's cram for the big test tomorrow.

Why didn't SpongeBob study hard for his driver's license test?

He didn't want to start a traffic cram.

Patrick: Where do tests come from?

Mrs Puff: The Exami-Nation.

Squidward: What makes you think Mrs Puff finds you clever?

Patrick: She said I have a smart mouth.

Mrs Puff: Knock-knock.
SpongeBob: Who's there?
Mrs Puff: Ann, sir.
SpongeBob: Ann sir who?
Mrs Puff: Answer the question, SpongeBob!

What's the difference between someone who do-si-dos and an idea from SpongeBob's head?

One's a square dancer and the other's a squared answer!

What electronic gadget did Patrick buy just before the big test?

An answering machine.

Sandy: What kind of answer doesn't belong in school?

Mrs Puff: A belly dancer!

SpongeBob: Why did the student write his maths homework on his toes?

Sandy: He was trying to think on his feet.

Why does Patrick think three, five, and seven are weird?

He heard they're odd numbers.

Why did Squidward sculpt a giant *A* out of clay?

He wanted to make the grade.

SpongeBob: What kind of test do they give in dancing school?

Squidward: True or waltz.

SpongeBob: What kind of test do they give in cooking school?

Mr Krabs: Multiple cheese.

Sandy: What's the difference between a trunk full of gold and a quiz on yellow cheese?

SpongeBob: One's a treasure chest and the other's a cheddar test.

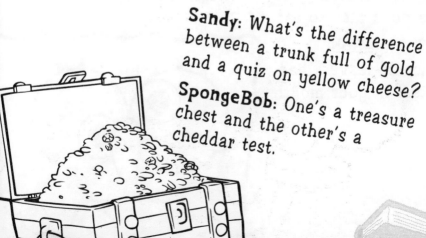

Why did SpongeBob bring a fly to school?

For shoo-and-tell.

Patrick: If you fail an exam, is it a good idea to eat it?

SpongeBob: No, it would leave a bad test in your mouth.

SpongeBob: Why do phones always sit in the front of the class?

Squidward: They love to be called on.

Sandy: How did the chicken improve her grades?

SpongeBob: She joined a study coop.

Why did Patrick bring slime to school?

For a goop project.

Why did Plankton bring a ladder to school?

He wanted to get high grades.

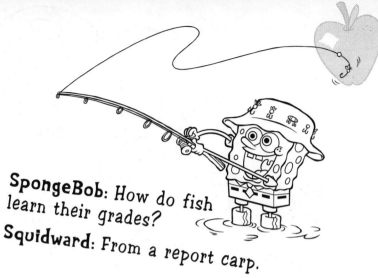

SpongeBob: How do fish learn their grades?

Squidward: From a report carp.

What book does Mr Krabs hate to take out?

His cheque book.

What did Patrick learn at school?

His ABZzzzzzzzz's.

What does SpongeBob write his homework on when he's at the beach?

Sandpaper.

Sandy: Why did the chicken cross the classroom?

Mrs Puff: To get eggs-tra credit.

Why did Patrick bring lots of pencils to gym class?

He wanted to end up with the most points.

What book does Mr Krabs love to study?

His bankbook.

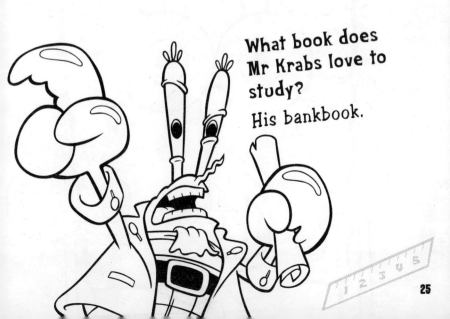

Why did one school bell always go off before the others?

It was the ringleader.

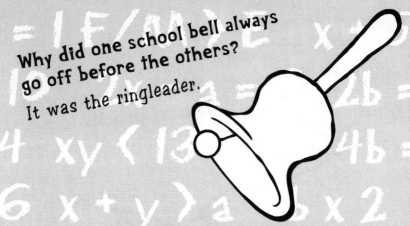

What did SpongeBob say when he realized he'd lost his oral report?

Nothing. He was speechless.

SpongeBob: Which fish is best in English class?

Mrs Puff: The grammarhead shark.

Why did SpongeBob's best friend take an apple to Mrs Puff?

He wanted to be teacher's Pat.

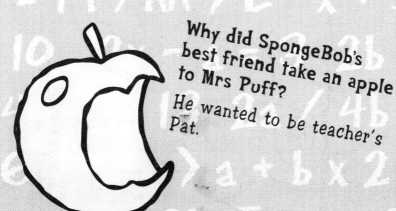

Why did Patrick build an extra room onto his rock?

His teacher told him to work on his addition.

Why did Patrick bring a seahorse to school?

He'd heard they were going to learn to read and ride.

What's the difference between a good student and Mr Krabs?

One knows how to read and the other's known for his greed.

Why did SpongeBob call his maths home-work a "mystery"?

It just didn't add up.

Sandy: Did the flying fish study the lesson on waves?

Patrick: He skimmed it.

Mr Krabs: Why do swordfish get good grades?

SpongeBob: Because they're sharp.

What did SpongeBob think of
Mr Krabs's lecture about pennies?

He couldn't make heads or tails
out of it.

When the teacher
asked him a question,
why did SpongeBob put
his hand in his mouth?

The answer was on the
tip of his tongue.

SpongeBob: How did the fish feel when school was cancelled?

Squidward: Like he was off the hook.

When does school turn Patrick's brain into a fish?

When it makes his head swim.

Why did Patrick lie down on the classroom floor?

The teacher told him to lower his voice.

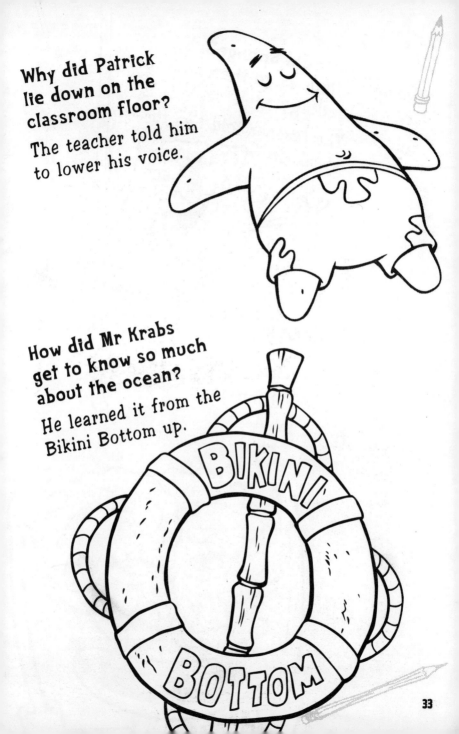

How did Mr Krabs get to know so much about the ocean?

He learned it from the Bikini Bottom up.

BIKINI BOTTOM

Why did SpongeBob climb up to the classroom ceiling?

The teacher told him to speak up.

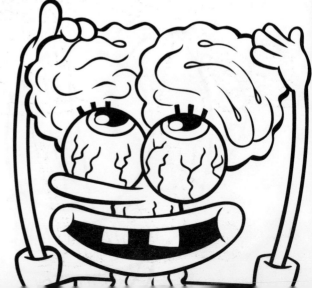

Why did SpongeBob wrap sheets and blankets around his brain?

The teacher told him to make up his mind.

Squidward: Why don't cows get exact answers in maths?

Sandy: They're always rounding up.

Why did Squidward spend hours talking about just one painting?

He wanted his students to get the picture.

Did Patrick play jump rope at recess?

He decided to skip it.

At fry-cook school did SpongeBob study for his grease exam?

No, he just let it slide.

SpongeBob: Why don't astronauts make good students?

Sandy: They keep spacing out.

Why did Patrick bring frozen orange juice to class?

The teacher told him he needed to concentrate.

Why did Plankton steal his chair from school?
The teacher told him to take his seat.

SpongeBob: What did the ghost get on his exam?

The Flying Dutchman: A Boo minus.

Squidward: What's the worst kind of *B* to get on your homework?

Patrick: A bumblebee.

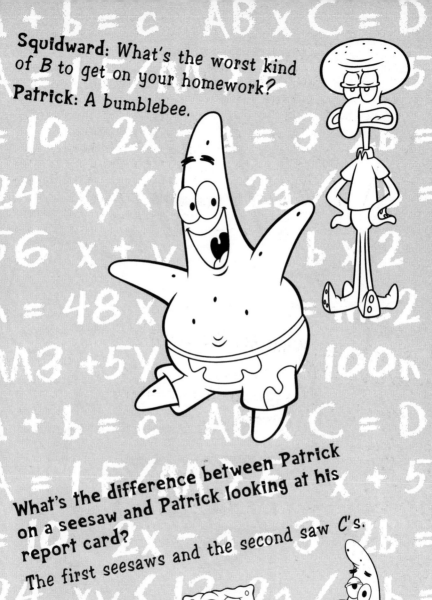

What's the difference between Patrick on a seesaw and Patrick looking at his report card?

The first seesaws and the second saw *C*'s.

What did Patrick say when he saw the teacher marking his test?

"Go ahead, make my D!"

SpongeBob: When is a D not a bad grade?
Sandy: When it's a chickadee.

Sandy: What did the dog get on his test?

Mr Krabs: An arf.

If Plankton were a grade, what grade would he be?

A-menace.

41

Patrick: Where do polar bears go after kindergarten?

SpongeBob: Frost grade.

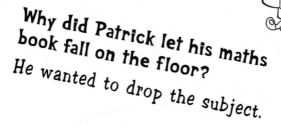

Why did Patrick let his maths book fall on the floor?

He wanted to drop the subject.

Sandy: Which grade is over the quickest?

Mrs Puff: Second grade.

Where did Sandy go after second grade?

Furred grade.

Where do bacteria have P. E. class?

In the germnasium.

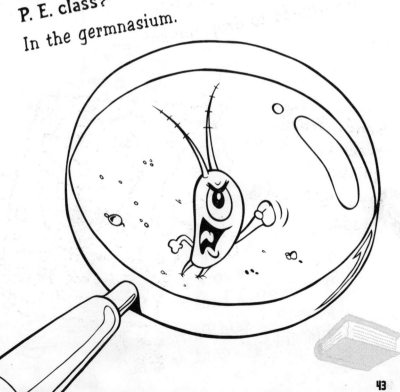

Which kind of musical note is Mr Krabs's favourite?

The quarter note.

Why did Patrick do his maths homework on SpongeBob's back?

SpongeBob said Patrick could always count on him.

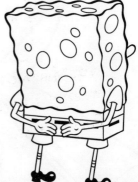

Why did Patrick hand in his test before he'd finished?

He ran out of guess.

Squidward: Was the school nurse willing to treat the sick sea monster?

Patrick: She said she'd give it a shot.

Why did SpongeBob do his school exercises over and over and over?

He wanted to be king of the drill.

What's Mr Krabs's favourite kind of test?

Fill-in-the-bank.

SpongeBob: Why do pirates make bad students?

Mr Krabs: Everything goes in one ahrrrr and out the other.

Patrick: Knock-knock.
SpongeBob: Who's there?
Patrick: Miss.
SpongeBob: Miss who?
Patrick: Mistakes are really easy to make.

Why can't Patrick divide by two?

He doesn't know the half of it.

SpongeBob: Is it hard to understand what "zero" means?

Patrick: Nah, there's nothing to it.

Patrick: Knock-knock.

SpongeBob: Who's there?

Patrick: Isabel.

SpongeBob: Isabel who?

Patrick: Is a bell ever going to end this school day?